Hey, Friend

Hey, Friend

Today, This Is What I'd Like to Say

Shirley Schwier

RESOURCE *Publications* · Eugene, Oregon

HEY, FRIEND
Today, This Is What I'd Like to Say

Resource Publications
An Imprint of Wipf and Stock Publishers
199 W. 8th Ave., Suite 3
Eugene, OR 97401

www.wipfandstock.com

PAPERBACK ISBN: 979-8-3852-3397-7
HARDCOVER ISBN: 979-8-3852-3398-4
EBOOK ISBN: 979-8-3852-3399-1

VERSION NUMBER 11/19/24

I dedicate this book to all interested readers. Even the ones who may not be interested at all.

This is for you!

To remind you that you are remembered.

You are not forgotten.

You are seen.

You are special.

And you have such a beautiful purpose here on earth.

Dream on, little dreamer.

Introduction

This book was written with the intention of reaching you.

You can enjoy the journey this book will take you on day to day, page by page, or consume it all in one sit-down.

You will be challenged to face a few realities of life and to overcome them. Truth will not be spoken in an obvious manner, but it is up to your own interpretation, insight, and discovery.

Let yourself be invited to a voyage of entertainment and small laughs, that by looking at the cover of this book once you have finished reading it, you remember what your takeaways were and how the words in this book have helped you be sent on your way!

You are loved. I hope you enjoy.

Hey, Friend

Did you not hear the phone ring again?

I left a voicemail.

I'll be sitting near the phone wondering if next time I should just abstain.

I bought a new coffee machine; it's blue, like you.

Deep and out of reach.

I love this machine. It keeps me company.

I've been thinking about nicknames lately, but it's been hard for me to think about names.

Anyways, you should come by sometime. For a cup, of course . . .

Oh, Friend

How can you be seven places all at once? Let me tell you how.

When the anger stirs up like a boiling pot, and the tears join in like bees swarming in.

The care, nurture we seek, not near, not within reach.

And at that moment when we cannot do more,

it. becomes. still.

That place where all we want is to be held in safety and in peace.

Sometimes it's loud, sometimes it's quiet. Devastation leaving us with nothing to speak.

Confusion, uncertainty, and deceit.

How could you take away what was most precious to me.

And How Would You Like Your Eggs?

Is the question that continues to spiral in my head.

Breakfast was my favorite time with you.

You'd open up the windows and enjoy the sound of the birds and light wind.

You always had to stay warm so lying where the sunlight was is your cozy and enjoyable sheltered place.

Just to stare at you once more, in your stillness.

What a blessing and a gift it was to see you during your truest stage. And so you answered, "Poached."

That's when I should've known.

And So, What Would You Like to Do Today?

Well, I like to listen to pop rock early Saturday mornings, maybe that's what I'll do today.

I like to walk two streets down to get my favorite coffee and donut.

I like the way we used to hold hands to walk down those two very busy streets.

Somehow holding your hand made that "not so long" walk a little sweeter.

To say my favorite flavored donut was discontinued hurts more, would be a dream. I'd trade that donut just to have you again.

I enter the shop, take my headphones out, and stop the pretend.

Change Is Scary, So I've Been Told

I can't seem to make sense of the why.

Weren't we the courageous ones?

The first ones to jump off the tallest challenge.

To hold our breaths for as long as the currents continued to drag us down.

What ever happened to being the adventurous ones?

Without being asked, willingly taking the chances against what we stumble upon in life.

Not hiding when the rocks are thrown.

I wonder what happened, because there's always a something that happens.

This time, kindly reply to Inertia that the invitation has been declined.

I Just Was Thinking . . .

About how much I miss braiding your long, thick,
and dark hair.

I've been riding the waves lately and scoping out the
challenges. About the things we want but not settling on
the things we can't have. The ones desired most.

One of those, which is you.

I wonder how different you look today.

People modernize nowadays to flee from who they used
to be.

But the hair? It's what drew me to you.

I think I'd love you anyhow. No matter the color or cut.

Because even after so long, if I ran into you, I'd still
recognize that it's you.

Hey, I Was Wondering,

When you're angry or upset, what is it that you do?

Do you blast music so loud you can feel your heart beat?

Do you drown in the hand-shaking silence wanting
to scream?

Do you sit still, feeling a little lost and confused?

In my anger, I lose it all.

In my hurt, I lose it all.

What's there to keep if every time I lose it all once
I turn green.

I've Got a Taste!

I figured it out . . . it's something in the reds.

Raspberry, Cherry

Pomegranate, and Strawberry.

The color is so appealing, it's never hard to miss.

Can I order this flavor please, all in one scoop.

Only if we could share one scoop . . . me one lick, you two.

Someone Said Will I Remember Their Name

I said, "It's not your name that is important."

More importantly, How did you make me feel?

My favorite memories are those that warm up my heart like a cup of hot chocolate.
The one-offs that I'll never encounter again.

The stranger at the stop light.

The kid waving through the glass.

The young lady complimenting my hair.

And the hands I couldn't reach.

Yours.

The brown-eyed stare.

Have We Gone Two Weeks Without Talking Again?

I don't want to adapt to the days that I'd go without talking to you. Just not yet.

But our dear friend, inevitable, invites itself in, and the chaos begins.

I understood that you must confront and not ignore.

The more you delay and act as if it were okay, it grows.

It grows in an area so large that no matter if you look left or right, it's in your face, and cannot be pushed away.

So, my choice? I choose the rain. I want to be cleansed. I give in.

Hey . . .

Turns out life WILL have it its way.

And there's nothing our feeble hands can do about it.

Like a Rubik's cube you cannot solve until you keep trying.

Having to learn what it is to live and figuring out if we're even doing it the right way.

Too many questions, not enough answers, only to realize enough answers were always there.

I just didn't accept them.

A Reminder of You

I saw a movie last night that reminded me of you.

The time we sneaked in through the back of "Uncle Nick's Most Favorite Picks." I bought you your first chocolate.

Hazelnuts, oh, hazelnuts . . . how good and tasteful you were to me.

Those treasures are hard to find, one of a kind.

Everything is closed nowadays.

If only I could find me one, just one, would I share it with you, my one of a kind.

Is It Trash Wednesdays at Your Place?

I think I missed mine.

I see everyone's trash put away. Why is it that mine is still full, unwilling to be moved?

I hope it is not a current representation of me.

Is there some cleaning that still needs to be?

You know what! I'll try to make it on time for next week's!

Or is that yet, another lie told unto me . . .

I said I wouldn't promise again if it were to be empty, but sometimes just hearing "I will do it" feels like enough.

When I can't do it, who can? Who will do it?

Hey, Guess What?

I waved at a dog today and it just stared dead at me.

I wonder why. I mean, I'm not a ghost.

But it does remind me of us.

By us I refer to the world. The living beings of the world who nowadays live very frothy.

I don't mean the froth that goes along with my lattes but what is inside of our hearts and minds.

There's just not much going on anymore. No more trying.

No more "it's the little things."

No more sparkle.

It's a bit of white, black, brown and beige. What ever happened to color?

I Just Wanted to Say . . .

My days are drifting away and so are yours.

Reflection is a bitter exercise.

Some say that's how you'll look back and appreciate what was but what if looking back takes you to a place that no longer exists, and it's where you want to be most.

To be there once more, again.

And so I take the train back to reality and admit, I have to stop looking back, because I am no longer there even if you are.

I have to join hope and expect a better tomorrow.

I am letting go of hurt and choosing a different disc to play.

Why Is It Easier to Share Instructions Than to Follow Them?

I learned a bit or two about submission.

When you're submitted, it is easy to follow.

But when you're not, it's like a professional dancing with an amateur.

Here, I'll lead.

All you have to do is follow and

F

  R   F

    E   A

     E   L

        L

Friend, Let Me Tell You What a Tuesday It Has Been!

I had to give up coffee.—The Sad End

Just kidding, more like just one cup a day.

Restraints, restraints, restraints . . .

For my health anyway.

I need to take care of myself so I can make it to the next days. I've got people to meet and places to see.

Folks to wave to, and a memory to keep. I bet it'll be exciting.

I Hope You Don't Remember Me

When we grow and become, we age and exist, in our definition of "Today." The me I used to be is no longer in me.

I will not be mad or sad if you cannot remember me.

The me that I used to be did not deserve to be next to you.

Not in that proximity.

My wish is that you forget. Forget it all and find that perfect place. Where tears do fall but of joy.

That you are shown care, attention, love, and a bit of thrill.

I hope you don't remember me at all.

Sometimes, I Just Hate Crying

Sometimes I hate my hair.

I hate not being left alone when I ask someone to "leave me alone."

I hate being frustrated.

And I hate, hating.

I eventually hate anything that disrupts peace.

Sometimes there's nothing I can do to protect it because life is not a choice. You have to live under the understanding that if you give up, that is it.

And so, I'm deciding to get over it.

Today wasn't my day. Tomorrow, could be.

I Would Like to Share a Secret

There's not the "perfect life" out there, whatever your plan is.

For every time you believe you have arrived, get ready, yet for another ride.

Sometimes, there are the highs and sometimes there are the lows.

But steady is not part of the plan.

That only exists in one place, and friend, neither you nor I have made it there yet.

I tell myself to buckle up. Every. Single. Day, for no matter what today may bring.

I find enjoyment in all things. In the good and in the hurt, and I'll tell you why. Because I get to feel. It proves that I am alive.

It proves I have been given a chance to experience this very life.

Mondays Are for Evenings

Well, because I don't get to see you till then. I wonder what you'll have for dinner.

I have pretzels, yogurt with granola, and for my sweet tooth, which always leads me to have dessert après le dîner, chocolate covered raisins.

Quite exquisite.

I miss you.

We should go to the park sometime. For,

A walk.

A kiss.

A scar.

Remember We'd Split Chores

The kitchen? It's my personal hiding place.

More like a personal laboratory if you ask me. You never know what you'll come out with.

I've been baking a lot.

A bit frustrating that I have not been able to master a treat.

I follow the recipes but they never "Wow" me. I sit there and think, "What could it be?"

I don't really know but I'll continue to take those leaps.

Talking about leaps . . . did you ever think you'd be hearing back from me?

But It's a New Day!

Hey, I was thinking about saying "hi" before it turns too late. I wanted to say that you are missed!

And I've been looking forward to life lately.

Not certain of what exactly but I am expectant.

I'm curious . . . I am excited!!

Anyways, I just wanted to share with you that I'm doing really good and soon, with hope, I'll get to where I'm supposed to be.

Whether that's near you or along the lines of never meant to be.

Make a Stop at 76th and Stanton

Cross.

Come, and cross with me.

I know you see the busy street but take my hand and trust in me.

I am not your harm so let me help you get there, to the where that you've always wanted to be.

I waved but you missed. I yelled and you didn't hear. I signaled but you ignored. Why did you let go of my hand?

And when things are no longer in our control, we pray because we've lost all hope.

Stay warm, friend. I'll remember this and know that my darkest days aren't so cold but full of grace.

What Ever Happened to That Dream?

The one that through the years continues to follow you.

The one that sometimes you forget about and then every once in a while it consumes you.

It ignites something in your mind, heart, and soul only for it to fade again due to lack of control.

Let it come to be. Invite it in, sit down and have some tea.

When your fingers crinkle, your tongue runs out of words and the excitement exceeds, go for it!

Don't hold yourself in, release, so that the person you are meets the one you are meant to be.

I'm thrilled for you my dearest friend, to see you make it and defeat what you had called "The End."

It's never really over until it finally is.

What It Does Mean

When you believe you are falling in love again . . .

Well, I don't choose to believe. Am I or am I not?

Hope.

To hope is all I have. That no matter what was dead to never grow again will bloom and embrace the untold story.

I think about Him sometimes. The one who helped.

He showed me what to look forward to even if I did not understand or comprehend.

But I believed! That it was meant to be.

And now as I smile, I ponder at what eventually came to be. A love story, between Him and me.

Can You Slow Down the Speed of the Turning Pages?

If not, let's open one of Life's.

Sing unto me and make me fall asleep. Wake me up
with gentleness and caress me.

Feed me with your love and let me go not.

Let me see your face daily and that I may not forget.
The face of he who pierced in me what love really means.

And so, every person desires that love.

The love that runs so deep the ocean is no longer out of reach.
The love that makes every smell seem so sweet!

Not focusing on the who, but just knowing that you are!

I Told Myself This Every Single Day

You are kind.

You are patient.

You are bright.

You are here to love others.

Others enjoy your company while you introduce them
to light. You make them want to relive it all again.

It's a moment of astonishment. And don't ask why.

Dismiss the small inconveniences and choose a good time.

You are here for not so a while, so plant what you'd like to
see so that one day you'll be able to reap.

So . . .

Tell me something new!

I know you have a few.

The things that you'll never get to share because we just aren't there.

Those things are okay.

The drift.

You have nothing to be scared of.

I'll make sure I hold on tight and don't let go from what keeps me grounded.

And when it gets cold and silent, not knowing where to go, I'll remember that your hands are all I know.

And How Thick Is This Page?

I've awaken during quite a few winter mornings, knowing that it wasn't winter at all. They felt and were so hopeless for as far as I could see.

Not knowing that Hope was always there, right next to me.

No wonder I woke up in tears yet showered.

No wonder my appetite was lost, yet I did not fade.

No wonder I am here today!

Because of He, who lives in me.

And so I move onto the afternoon and look forward to what this evening may bring.

www.ingramcontent.com/pod-product-compliance
Lightning Source LLC
Chambersburg PA
CBHW060643030426
42337CB00018B/3426